KTG know the game

Billiards
and
Snooker

Produced in collaboration with
The Billiards and Snooker Control Council

Published by A & C Black (Publishers) Ltd
35 Bedford Row, London WC1R 4JH

Contents

Photographs inside front cover (Cliff Thorburn) and
page 2 (Dennis Taylor) courtesy of David Muscroft

Foreword

In these modern times when hustle and bustle seem to be the keywords to our very existence, it is not surprising to find that as a form of relaxation the games of billiards and snooker are beginning to enjoy a popularity reminiscent of some 35 years ago, when other distractions were not quite so numerous as today.

Billiards, to the enthusiast, offers a lifetime of study in technique and a variation of moods unsurpassed by any other ball game. Its limits are unending, and until one has persevered and achieved some measure of success these pleasures are not experienced or so easily come by.

Snooker, on the other hand, enjoys far greater popularity and offers a quicker reward for your efforts. The coloured balls with fifteen reds are very inviting, and games are of shorter duration than billiards; the players, being only concerned with potting balls, get the idea of the game quickly and, according to their natural ability, their enthusiasm grows. As improvement progresses, so new moves become apparent, and extremely high standards can be achieved.

With the vast number of people now coming into contact with both games, this booklet has been produced to enlighten the uninitiated and put them on the right road to what can be a most enjoyable pastime or, indeed, an extremely competitive sport at whatever level one's ability allows, involving all the social pleasantries that run parallel to the game. This booklet undoubtedly fulfils the purpose for which it was written, and will, I am sure, help all its readers to further their pleasure from two such wonderful games.

W. H. COTTIER
Chairman,
Billiards and Snooker
Control Council
1972-81

Since the foregoing was written by my predecessor, interest in the games, particularly snooker, has increased beyond all expectations. The vast amount of television coverage has undoubtedly made its contribution.

Snooker centres are opening throughout the United Kingdom, providing new opportunities for ladies and young people to participate, which they are doing in ever-increasing numbers.

Our staff will help wherever possible. Many happy hours to you all.

STAN BROOKE
Chairman,
Billiards and Snooker
Control Council

Historical introduction

The origin of billiards is rather indefinite, and no country can really claim to have founded the game: the evidence is too conflicting to convince.

Early in the seventeenth century, however, many specific references were made to a rudimentary form of the game; and in England such allusions are plentiful. Spenser refers to the game in his *Mother Hubberds Tale*, 1591, and as early as 1576 Mary Queen of Scots, then a state prisoner, complained she had been deprived of her billiard table. In 1634 one of the quaint engravings illustrating the *Divine Emblems* of Francis Quarles depicts a form of billiards with maces instead of cues. James I ordered a 'billiarde bourde' in 1605 or thereabouts. References were also made by such famous authors as Ben Jonson (1637), Evelyn (1674) and Dr Johnson (1775). In France, Louis XIV favoured the game.

The modern form of billiards dates from the early nineteenth century, and the first serious English treatise is that of E. White, published in 1807. The first professional champion of any account was Jonathan Kentfield, who published a book on the game in 1839. In 1849 he relinquished his title to John Roberts, Senior, father of the great John Roberts (Junior). Great professionals since the Roberts' era have included H. Stevenson, C. Dawson, M. Inman, T. Reece, W. Lindrum, J. Davis, T. Newman, W. Smith, C. McConachy, C. Falkiner and many more.

The Amateur Billiards Championship originated in 1888, and it is now the chief event of the billiards season. So far as match-play is concerned, snooker has ousted billiards to a great extent in the professional sphere. Its origin, however, is fairly recent and well authenticated. It is a development of 'Black Pool', and was first played in Jubbulore, India, in 1875, when English army officers added several coloured balls to the existing 15 reds and the black.

The term 'snooker' was a slang word for first-year cadets at the R.M.A. Woolwich. Sir Neville Chamberlain, then a lieutenant in the Devonshire Regiment, used the expression in addressing a colleague who had left the cue-ball behind a colour when a red was the next ball 'on'. He then had to explain the word to the company, adding that they were all, so to speak, snookers, and it might be an appropriate name for the game.

The equipment

The table

Billiards is a game of skill played with three balls and a cue on an eight-legged table that has six pockets. Snooker is played on the same table with similar equipment, but twenty-two balls are used. Snooker originated from Pyramids and Pool, both of which it has superseded. As far as technique is concerned, every shot in snooker is part of billiards technique. For both games, the balls must be equal in size and weight, measuring 52.5mm ($2\frac{1}{16}$ inches) in diameter. Today, most balls are made of crystalate, which displaced ivory during the late 1920s.

The cue, which must not be less than 910mm (3 feet) long, is usually about 1.5m (4 feet 10 inches), and consists of a tapering piece of wood, generally ash. The butt-end (held in the hand) is a little over 25mm (one inch) wide, and the cue gradually tapers to a round top, on which a leather tip is glued. With this end the player strikes the ball, the tip being approximately 10mm to 12mm in diameter. A piece of special chalk is necessary for roughening the surface of the tip after two or three strokes, as otherwise the tip would slide off when it came into contact with the polished surface of the ball. The length of a cue, its weight, and the size of the tip vary according to the preference of the player. The balance of the cue is mainly achieved by weighting the butt. The player's other hand forms a 'bridge' for the cue on the table surface.

The table stands 2 feet $9\frac{1}{2}$ inches to 2 feet $10\frac{1}{2}$ inches from the floor and its slate bed measures 12 feet long by 6 feet $1\frac{1}{2}$ inches wide. This slate bed is incorporated in an elaborate wooden frame, the bed being covered with a tightly-stretched green woollen cloth, which has a thickish nap, running from the bottom to the top end of the table. There are six pockets, one at each corner, and one exactly in the middle of each long side. Resilient rubber cushions, overhanging no more than 2 inches and no less than $1\frac{1}{2}$ inches, enclose the playing area. There is, of course, a gap in the cushion at each place where a pocket is situated, to allow the ball to enter.

The above dimensions are those of the full-size standard table whose measurements are defined in imperial units.

The marking of the table

The playing area is marked in the following way:

A line is drawn across the width of the table parallel with the bottom cushion and 740mm (29 inches) from its face. This is called the 'baulk line', and the space within it is 'baulk'. From the centre point of this line, a semi-circle is marked within the baulk area with a radius of 290mm ($11\frac{1}{2}$ inches). This is called the 'D'. When the player is 'in hand' – that is, when his ball is off the table before starting the game, or after his ball has entered a pocket – he must take his next stroke from the 'D' area. Any point may be chosen, either on the baulk line, or within the semi-circular area.

The other markings consist of four 'spots' on the imaginary central longitudinal line of the table. These

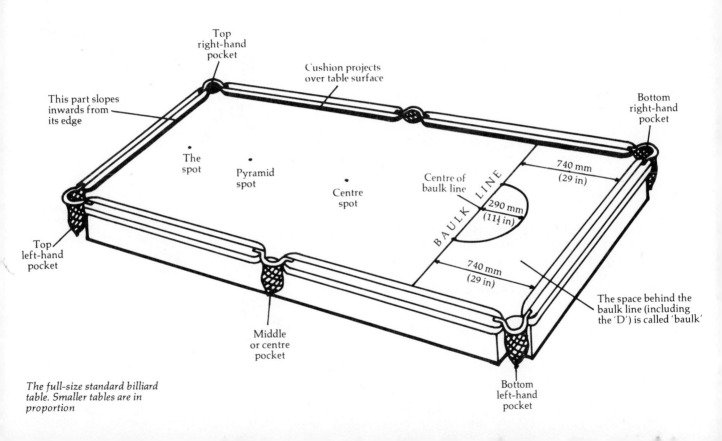

Top right-hand pocket

Cushion projects over table surface

Bottom right-hand pocket

This part slopes inwards from its edge

The spot

Pyramid spot

Centre spot

Centre of baulk line

BAULK LINE

740 mm (29 in)

290 mm (11¼ in)

Top left-hand pocket

740 mm (29 in)

The space behind the baulk line (including the 'D') is called 'baulk'

Middle or centre pocket

Bottom left-hand pocket

The full-size standard billiard table. Smaller tables are in proportion

spots, marked with very small wafer-like pieces of silk, or by chalk, are positioned as follows:
○ At the centre of the baulk line.
○ At the centre of the table itself (the 'centre spot').
○ Halfway between the centre spot and the face of the top cushion (the 'pyramid spot').
○ 324mm (12¾ inches) from the face of the cushion (the 'spot').

The rests

There are certain 'positions' in which favourable access to the cue-ball is difficult. For these, a 'rest' is provided. A metal or plastic cross at the end of the rest forms a bridge, and different lengths of rest are available. The short, or 'half-butt' rest is 2.4m (8 feet) long, while the 'long rest' is 3.6m (12 feet) long. A long cue is provided for each of these rests. There are also positions in which the player cannot easily contact his cue-ball because another ball is close to it. To cope with this difficulty, the player uses the 'spider' rest, providing a bridge of extra height with a long handle like the other rests.

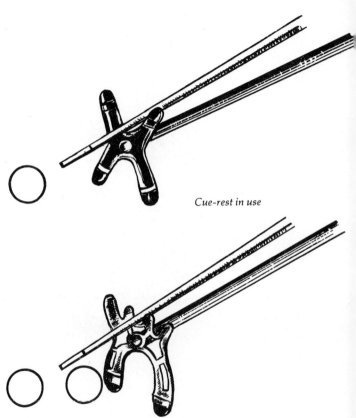

Cue-rest in use

'Spider' in use

How to play

The stance for both games
The stance shown here is ideal, though the height and physical characteristics of different people will often make minor variations necessary. Tall players obviously have more difficulty in obtaining the ideal stance than those of short or medium height.

(a) Left leg thrust forward and slightly bent; right leg more or less at right angles to it; both feet firmly planted; weight equally distributed between the two feet; body inclined easily and comfortably.

Jack Karnehm, National Coach, Billiards and Snooker Foundation

(b) Head well down, as near as possible to an ideal position in which the cue touches, or almost touches, the chin.
(c) Left arm as straight as possible out on the table.
(d) Right forearm perpendicular.
(e) Eyes looking straight along the cue in its course towards the ball.
(f) Cue-action as near to absolute horizontal as possible; its movement should be piston-like.
(g) The 'bridge', the position assumed by the hand on which the cue is resting, must be firm, with the fingers gripping the cloth. A 'looped' bridge, widely used in the American and Continental games, can be used to advantage in particular circumstances.
(h) The cue should move freely, without deviation to either side; the fewer to-and-fro motions used, the better.

The ordinary bridge

The 'looped' bridge

Forms of striking

(a) *Plain striking:* hitting the cue-ball dead centre.

(b) *Top:* hitting the cue-ball high up promotes extra forward rotation; contact is between top and centre.

(c) *Bottom:* hitting the cue-ball low down (i.e. halfway between bottom and centre) retards forward motion.

(d) *Stab:* a sharp, stunning stroke, to make the cue-ball stop dead and remain on the spot previously occupied by the object-ball.

Stun: similar to stab, a heavy, deadening stroke used by a player who wishes to leave the cue-ball nearby after contact.

(e) *Screw:* hitting the cue-ball low and with follow-through motion, causing it to take an angle less than the natural angle after contact.

Screw-back: the same kind of stroke, but intended to give a direct recoil or backward motion towards the striker.

The diagrams in Fig. 1 do not represent specific strokes: they simply give a rough idea of the effect of each technical feature, taking the plain strike, (a), as the norm. So here (b) shows the extra momentum given to the cue-ball by 'top', (c) shows the decreased momentum when 'bottom' is applied, (d) shows the effect of stun and stab, which cause the cue-ball to stop nearby, and (e) shows how the cue-ball recoils in a screw-back stroke.

Fig. 2 shows the course of the cue-ball in the right-angle screw cannon, half-ball contact. For an

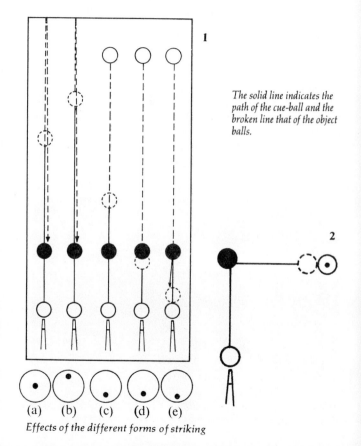

The solid line indicates the path of the cue-ball and the broken line that of the object balls.

Effects of the different forms of striking

explanation of the half-ball shot, turn to p.16.

(f) *Side:* hitting the cue-ball on its right or left side to increase or decrease the throw-off of the half-ball stroke. Travelling with the nap, the cue-ball veers appreciably in the direction of the side, and the deviation increases when contact is made with the object-ball. *Against* the nap, right-hand side results in a slight veering of the cue-ball to the left. To apply side, keep the cue straight as in plain striking.

Suppose the object-ball to be on the centre spot, and the cue-ball on the centre-spot of the 'D'. Imagine that the player intends to make a half-ball contact on the right-hand side of the object-ball. In this case right (or 'running') side will cause the cue-ball to deviate from the object-ball at a *wider* angle than the half-ball angle; however, left (or 'check') side will cause it to deviate at an angle *narrower* than the half-ball angle.

In diagram 1 'with the nap', the broken line shows the path of a plain half-ball stroke, and the solid line that of a stroke with running side (i.e. right-hand). Notice how running side increases the 'throw-off' of the half-ball stroke. Diagram 2 shows how check side (here also right-hand) decreases the half-ball throw-off, with the solid line representing the check side stroke. In diagram 1 check side would be left-hand side.
Running side increases the half-ball angle.

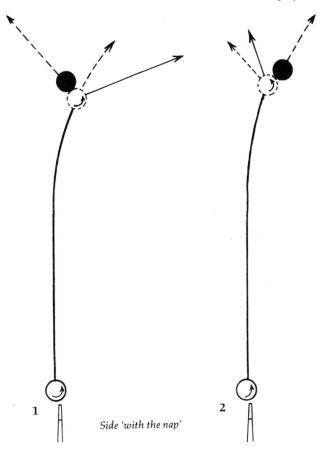

1

2

Side 'with the nap'

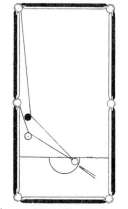

Short and Long Jenny

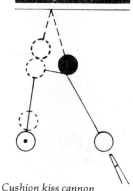

Cushion kiss cannon

Check side decreases the half-ball angle.

Pocket side is that side which carries the cue-ball into the pocket if it strikes the pocket jaw in a 'losing hazard' (see pp.14 and 16).

(g) *Strokes combining side with top or bottom.* While plain striking suffices for a large number of strokes, side and its attributes (i.e. top, bottom, stab, stun, drag etc) are essential for many others, and are often employed in combinations. Two of the commonest combinations are drag and side, and screw and side, but such matters belong to the advanced aspects of the game.

Drag: hitting the cue-ball low, as well as using the requisite side, to make it slither and travel a distance before the side operates. If the object-ball is near the top end, drag is used to ensure true running, and since drag retards the pace of the cue-ball the strength used should not be excessive. Remember that the aim is to ensure a given position of the balls after the stroke, and excessive force scatters them.

Drag is also employed with side in two strokes that often recur, the Short and the Long Jenny. The diagram illustrates them both. The drag, combined with pocket side (in this case left, or check), helps to maintain the side, which causes the cue-ball to curl inwards towards the pocket opening.

Masse stroke: a stroke that imparts a kind of side; achieved by striking the top area of the cue-ball with uplifted cue, causing the ball to travel in a curve.

Swerve: hitting the cue-ball with the cue tilted at an angle, causing it to swerve. Often used in billiards; in snooker it can cause the cue-ball to swerve around a ball intervening between the cue-ball and the ball the player intends to contact.

(h) *Miscellaneous shots*

Full ball contact: causes the cue-ball to contact the object-ball dead in the middle.

Fine stroke or 'cut': a glancing stroke just contacting the 'outside edge' of the object-ball.

Kiss cannon: the commonest form is a cushion kiss cannon (see diagram). 'In the open', however, the cue-ball contacts the first object-ball, causing it to 'kiss' the second, which is in its turn overtaken and contacted by the cue-ball.

The art of playing
The art of playing consists of:
(a) attaining a high standard of stroke play; in other words, perfecting the ability to perform the various types of stroke.
(b) ball-control; that is, making a scoring stroke with the necessary degree of strength and accuracy to ensure a favourable position for another scoring stroke. A favourable position for scoring is called a 'good leave'; an unfavourable one, a 'bad leave'.

Indifferent players hit too hard and concern themselves mainly with scoring. Good players concentrate mainly on the leave, since they take the score for granted. If the player's technique is such that every stroke appears easy to the onlooker (causing him to think, for instance, that 'I could do any of the strokes'!) then he can be said to be playing high-class billiards or snooker.

Artistry involves accuracy and nicely-gauged ball control, and results in a 'break': a chain of interrelated strokes, each leading to the next.

The referee
As in other games, a referee superintends the play and is the sole judge of conformity to, or infringements of, the rules. In major games he is assisted by a marker who controls the scoreboard. The referee not only ensures adherence to the rules, but takes the balls out of the pockets for the players, and 'spots' or returns them to the player at the baulk-end as necessary. He always calls the score after each stroke; it is the player's responsibility to ensure that the score is correctly recorded.

The referee must declare all fouls directly he perceives them. If he has not seen a foul stroke fully, he may ask nearby spectators for confirmation of the occurrence in question.

He must be careful not to obstruct the player's line of vision, facility of stroke etc.

A player may seek the referee's decision on certain points specified in the rules. He may not ask him for what amounts to advice or assistance.

Billiards

The game
Three balls are used in billiards, one red and two white.

Each player (there are normally only two) takes one of the white balls. One of these white balls is marked with a black spot at each of its two 'poles', or extremities. This is called the 'spot' ball, or simply 'spot'; the other white ball is called 'plain'.

How the game is played
To decide which player takes spot, and which plain, both either toss up or 'string' for the privilege, though apart from personal fancy there is no real advantage in playing with one ball or the other. However, winning the toss or 'string' does give the winner the choice of ball and of playing first, or of requesting his opponent to do so.

To 'string', each player directs a white ball from the baulk line to the top cushion, with the object of causing it to remain as near the bottom cushion as possible. To do this, the ball may reach the bottom cushion and rebound. The player whose ball remains nearer to the cushion wins the string.

Length of game
There are two systems governing the length of a game:
(a) The winner is the player who reaches a fixed number of points (e.g. 100, 250, 500 etc.).
(b) The winner is the player who leads after a certain period of time has expired (e.g. one hour, two hours, or four hours in two two-hour sessions).

Scoring
The object of the game is to score more points than your opponent. The cue-ball must be struck with the cue-tip and not pushed; a push is a foul. A player who makes a scoring stroke may then take another stroke, and so on until he fails to score; this is called a 'break'. Points are scored by three types of stroke:
(a) *The cannon.* A cannon is scored by the player striking his ball with his cue-tip (the player's ball is called the 'cue-ball') and causing it to contact the other two balls, i.e. the opponent's white (called the 'object-white') and the red, or vice versa, in turn. Two points. Successive cannons are limited to 75 in number.
(b) *The losing hazard, 'loser', or 'in-off'.* A losing hazard is made by striking the cue-ball and causing it to enter a pocket after contact with one of the

other two balls. A 'loser' off the object-white scores two points; off the red ball, three. These are known respectively as a 'white loser' and a 'red loser'.

(c) *The winning hazard, or 'pot'*. A winning hazard is made by striking the cue-ball to contact one of the two object-balls and cause the object-ball to enter a pocket. For 'potting' the white, the player scores two points; for potting the red, three. Successive hazards, winning or losing, are limited to fifteen.

A player pots the white for defensive purposes only; when it enters a pocket it stays off the table until the opponent plays, so limiting the possibilities of further scoring. The red ball, however, is placed on the spot after being potted.

In all diagrams, the broken lines indicate the paths of the object-balls, and the solid line that of the cue-ball.

It is possible to score a cannon and a losing hazard, or a winning hazard (pot), or even both, in the same stroke; but such combinations are generally 'flukes' (accidental shots). However, in a few

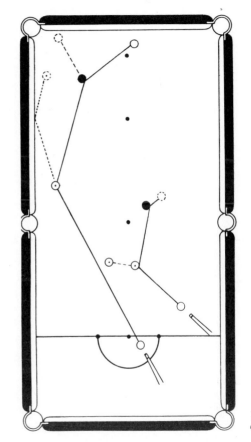

The cannon: the cue-ball contacts white, then red

Left: *The losing hazard: the cue-ball contacts red and then enters the middle pocket. The stroke used here is the basic stroke of the game, the 'half-ball' shot, in which the player aims through the centre of the cue-ball at the outer rim of the object-ball. From this angle, countless others are estimated: a skill that is soon learned by practice. 'Side' (striking right or left of the cue-ball's centre) increases or reduces the half-ball angle*

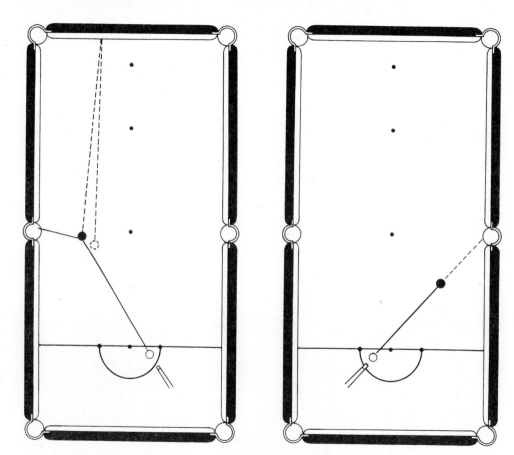

Right: *The winning hazard: the player directs the red into the middle pocket, his cue-ball coming to rest near the pocket*

instances a five- or six-shot is profitable. If a player makes a cannon and a losing or winning hazard on one stroke, he scores two points for the cannon. For the hazard he scores two if the white ball was struck first in the cannon, and three if it was the red ball. The most common 'combination' shot is that in which the player pots the red and follows in (a loser) with the cue-ball so he can get into the 'D'. This shot scores six points.

The total number of points scored by a player after a series of scoring strokes is called a 'break'; e.g. a break of 50, or a 50-break.

The player is not obliged to try to score; an unfavourable position of the balls may suggest a defensive stroke. When a player fails to make a scoring stroke in the course of his turn at the table, his turn ceases, and his opponent then takes his turn.

The opening shots

At the beginning of the game, the red ball is placed on the spot and the opponent's ball is 'in hand', and therefore not on the table.

The player starting the game places his

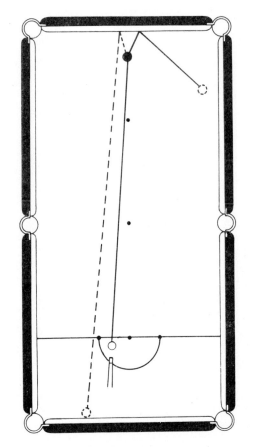

A recognized opening shot

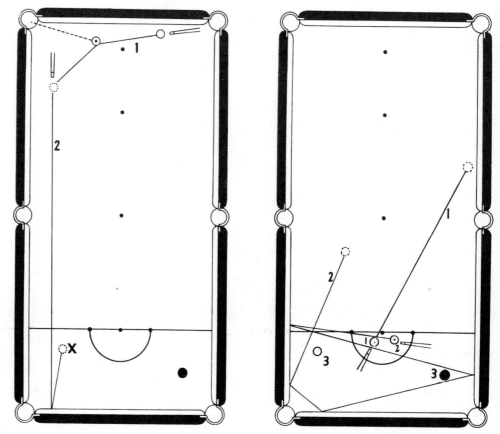

A miss is a foul stroke unless the striker is in hand and there is no ball out of baulk.
Left: *a miss (after potting white) made to put the cue-ball in position for a red loser. This is against the above rule.*
Right: *here the miss (stroke 1) is in order, as the striker is in hand and there is no ball out of baulk. Stroke 2 tries to disturb the red, but fails, and the opponent is left with the red in a good position for the losing hazard*

ball in the 'D', wherever he chooses, and must then direct it out of baulk. His aim should be to put both balls into baulk, so denying the second player a ball to play at.

Note. The left-hand spot of the 'D' is not used in billiards; the right-hand spot is used in only one case (see Rule 7).

The baulk area

When a player is in hand (i.e., when his ball is off the table) he must play from some point within the 'D', away from baulk and not directly into it. If one or both of the object-balls is in the baulk area, it cannot be played at directly. Note that a ball is in baulk when it rests on the baulk line, or between the baulk line and the bottom cushion.

If no chance of a score exists, then the player can win an advantage, and the initiative, by potting the white ball and placing the red and the cue-ball in baulk. If his opponent then fails to disturb either ball by his stroke out of baulk, the player may have a scoring stroke left.

The red is the more important of the two object-balls for the simple reason that it counts for three rather than two, and must always be replaced on the table after it has been pocketed. The object-white, as already noted, stays in the pocket if it is potted until the opponent's turn arrives or until fifteen hazards have been made. 'Losing the white' is a major handicap unless it forms an intentional part of a defensive tactic, as afterwards the player has only the red left. The white is often lost unintentionally.

When the red is pocketed it must be replaced on the spot. The same applies if the red is forced off the table (which is a foul). If the spot is occupied by another ball, the red must be replaced on the pyramid spot; and if that spot is occupied, on the centre spot. If the red is pocketed twice in succession from the spot or from the pyramid spot, it must be placed on the centre spot. The rules refer to other contingencies, but these are the basic principles.

When a ball is forced off the table, the next player may play from the position left, or he may opt to have the balls spotted. Every time the cue-ball enters a pocket, the player then 'in hand' goes to the bottom end of the table and plays from the 'D'.

If the striker's ball remains touching another ball, the red is placed on the spot, the non-striker's ball (if on the table) is placed on the centre spot, and the striker plays from hand.

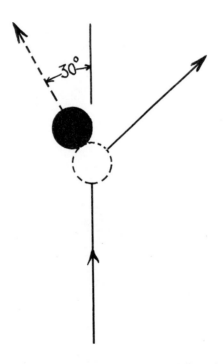

A half-ball shot

A stroke that does not contact another ball is a 'miss'; this is a foul except when the striker is in hand and there is no ball out of baulk. Every foul incurs a penalty of two points, which is added to the opponent's score.

Types of play

(a) *Losing hazard or 'loser' play:* the kind of play most favoured by amateurs. The player aims to make as many losing hazards as he can, with cannons and pots to leave such strokes when a loser is not practicable. It is a combination of hazards (losing and winning) and cannons.

The 'half-ball shot' is the basis of losing hazard play. The player aims at the outside edge of the object-ball through the centre of his ball (the cue-ball). This stroke is subject to variations, where a fuller or lesser contact is made according to the position of the object-ball; sometimes the player has to 'run through' the object-ball, causing his ball to take the object-ball very thickly and pass over the space it occupied.

(b) *Close-cannon play or 'nursery cannons':* a form of cannon play where the player scores a sequence of cannons with the three balls close to the cushions. Not more than 75 'direct' cannons must be made, as already stated. Very few players can master this play and 'in the open', away from the cushions, sequences of more than three or four cannons are rarely made.

(c) *'Top-of-the-table play':* a combination of pots of the red ball and cannon play, with the spot as the focal point of the strategy. This, for instance, is a favourite 'top-of-the-table' position:

The player cannons, sends the red ball towards the opposite pocket for a pot, and then tries to leave another cannon of similar type from the other side of the table. This alternate pot and cannon play is extremely difficult, however; generally an extra pot from the spot, or a second cannon, comes into the scheme. Top-of-the-table play is much more difficult than the all-round 'open' or 'loser' game.

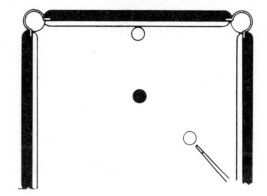

A good 'top-of-the-table' position

Fouls exclusive to billiards
(For fouls common to both billiards and snooker, see p.34).

(a) If a player plays his ball into baulk when in hand, and fails to come out of baulk.

(b) If the player plays a miss – unless he is in hand and there is no ball out of baulk.

(c) If a foul is awarded by the referee, the opponent has the option of playing from the position of the balls left as a result of the foul, or of having the balls spotted and playing from hand.

(d) If the player plays with the wrong ball.

Example of a break in billiards

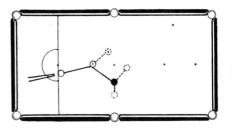

1. *Soft cannon to leave another: 2 points*

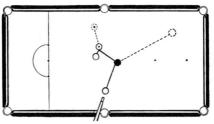

2. *Cannon, to send white near middle pocket for a loser, and red towards top pocket: 4 (total)*

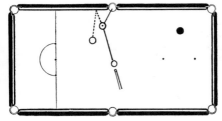

3. *White loser into middle pocket, to leave cannon: 6. (This loser is an example of the 'run-through' stroke)*

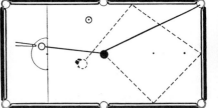

7. *Long loser, fairly forceful, to get red near white; red, however, though well down table, is on opposite side to white. So a further stroke must be made to bring it near white: 17*

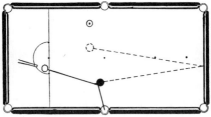

8. *Another middle pocket loser, this time hard enough to bring red to white: 20*

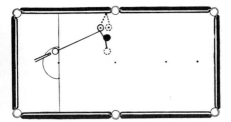

9. *A soft cannon but white still left unfavourable, as one does not want to pot it and a loser off it is not practicable: 22*

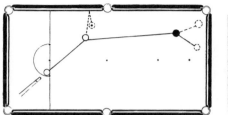

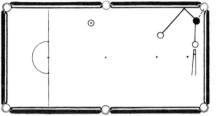

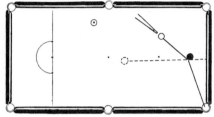

4. *Cannon off white, to drive red near pocket (gentle stroke): 8*

5. *Pot red (which is replaced on billiard spot) to leave loser into opposite top pocket: 11*

6. *Loser off red to bring red down table near white to rescue white from unfavourable position, but inadequate strength used: 14*

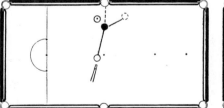

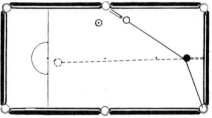

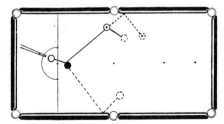

10. *Red potted to leave loser off red on its spot: 25. (Note: The strokes in this break do not represent the policy of an advanced player)*

11. *Loser off red, on the billiard spot, at last bringing red down table for a cannon which will rescue the white: 28*

12. *The cannon is made bringing white out from the cushion, making a white loser possible, and red also is left favourable. Thirty points scored and position perfect for continuing*

Snooker

The game

Where billiards offers three ways of scoring, snooker has only one: the winning hazard. In short, it is a 'potting' game. The other important and characteristic element is 'snookering', which is a means of obstructing your opponent. So far as technique is concerned, every shot in snooker is part of billiards technique.

Few good billiard players care for four-handed billiards (two against two), but four-handed snooker is immensely popular: snooker has less continuity and each player's turn comes more frequently.

The baulk area has no significance in snooker; the baulk-line, apart from that portion forming part of the 'D', appears on the table only because it is relevant to billiards. The 'D' serves the same purpose as it does in billiards: the player plays from within it when he is in hand, that is, after the cue-ball has entered a pocket (which is a foul). At the start of the game, too, the first player plays from the 'D'. In snooker, the ball may be played in any direction from the 'D'.

Right: *starting position*

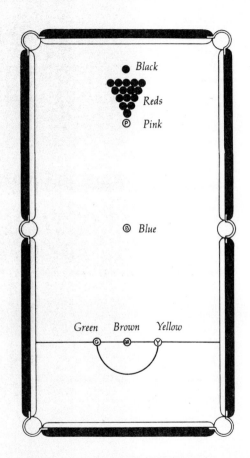

Twenty-two balls are used. These are the cue-ball, which each player uses in turn, fifteen red balls and six 'pool' or coloured balls, known as the 'colours'. These are yellow, green, brown, blue, pink and black.

The balls are placed, or set up, in the manner shown in the diagram. The fifteen red balls form a pyramid or triangular pack (hence the expression 'to break the pack', or disturb the opening formation of red balls). The six colours go on their respective spots as shown. A triangular wooden frame, the 'triangle', enables the reds to be set up as shown. The apex red should be as near as possible to the pink without touching it.

The object of the game is to pot all the balls in succession, as follows. A red ball is potted first, then any colour, then another red, then again a colour, and so on until all fifteen reds are pocketed. The reds remain in the pocket each time they are potted, but a colour is retrieved from the pocket and replaced on its spot each time. Consequently, after all the red balls have been cleared from the table, the six colours remain. These must then be potted in the following order: yellow, green, brown, blue, pink, black. This time each colour remains in the pocket when it has been potted. After the black is disposed of, the game is finished. The winner is the player who has gained the higher number of points. Points are scored as follows: for potting a red ball – one point; for potting yellow – two; green – three; brown – four; blue – five; pink – six; black – seven.

Such a game is called a 'frame' (of snooker), and a match consists of a given number of frames, which may be anything from the 'best of three frames' up to – say – the best of 141, lasting two weeks, as used to be the custom in some big professional contests.

General strategy of snooker

The chief aim, of course, is to pot the balls, and some players simply concentrate on potting without worrying about leaving the balls 'left' (favourably placed) for their opponent if they miss. Potters of exceptional ability, therefore, go all out to pot the balls as quickly as possible, but they often come to grief against a calculating player who sets out to make things difficult for them by leaving the cue-ball in awkward positions, and by laying snookers whenever possible. Two or three skilful defensive shots, including a snooker or two, will often bring a player a winning opening. Some players are supremely gifted in potting, and when their eye is in they can win a frame in no time; but the best players are those who combine good potting with calculated craft and tactics, and await their opportunities.

Positional play is all-important in snooker, and success lies in the ability to pot a ball and get into perfect position to pot the next ball. In doing so, the player may have to pot a red at the bottom end and get to the other end for position on a colour. He must do this in such a way that he does not collide with other

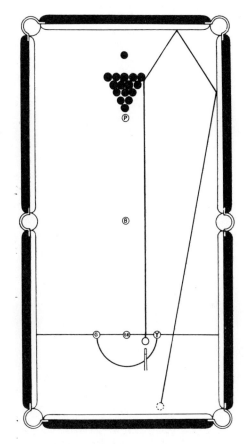

balls. This means that a knowledge of the 'angles' – the contacts with the cushions – is indispensable.

Example of a break

The player pots a red (1), then blue (5), total 6 – another red (1), total 7 – then pink (6), total 13 – another red (1), total 14 – green (3), total 17 – a red again (1), total 18 – the black (7), total 25 – and then misses a red pot. Break 25, and his opponent takes his turn, being on a red and playing from the position left.

To be 'on' a ball means that ball is the one the player may 'lawfully' play at; for instance, when reds are on the table, each time a player takes his turn he is 'on' a red; once he has potted it, he is 'on' a colour. Each time a player fails to score (by potting a ball on) his opponent takes his place at the table.

The highest possible normal break at snooker is 147; 15 reds (15 points) and 15 blacks (105), making 120, plus the colours $(2+3+4+5+6+7 = 27)$.

The opening shots

The two favourite methods of opening the game are shown here. No. 1 is still favoured by a small number of amateurs. No. 2 is the most usual professional stroke, and the majority of good amateurs also adopt it. The advantage of No. 2 is that the cue-ball, because it crosses the table, is more likely to remain on or near the bottom cushion; this achieves the desired aim of making things awkward for the opponent. It is also less likely to collide with any of the three bottom colours.

No. 1 can be made without side (see p.11). No. 2 needs a fair amount of right-hand side and is, therefore, more difficult. The stroke can also be made on the left of the pack, of course.

No. 1 makes thin contact on the end red of the five-group, generally returning to baulk right of the yellow, as shown. Too thick contact may cause brown to be hit on the return. The object, as stated, is to lie on or near the bottom cushion, or (if rebounding off the cushion) behind one of the three 'D' colours.

No. 2 contacts the end of the second row (the four-group). There are two risks to guard against:
(a) If the red is hit too thinly, the blue may be hit on the return journey.

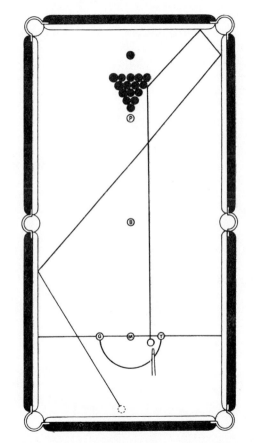

2

Opening shot

(b) If the red in front (in the three-group) is also hit, the cue-ball may go into the top pocket (a foul).

As no ball can be potted, except by accident, the object of both strokes is to leave the opponent as awkwardly placed as possible when he takes his turn.

Snookering

Snookering, which gives the game its name, is so important that its significance must be understood at the outset. A player is 'snookered' when he is prevented from hitting either side of all balls on by a direct stroke because of obstruction by another ball which is not on.

In each case, the only way the opponent can 'get out of the snooker' is to play off one or more cushions. However, in doing so he is very likely to hit a ball that is not on, or miss altogether, thereby suffering a penalty and offering a good opening to the player who laid the snooker.

Snookering is an integral part of the game. It is 'defensive tactics', but as it can lead to an opening it may legitimately be called offensive. A player who ties up his opponent with one, two or more such strokes wins the initiative, while his opponent's efforts to escape simply land him in further difficulties.

Safety shots

Snookering is not the only defensive or tactical play. If you cannot snooker, there is another stroke you can use to make things awkward for your opponent. This involves sending the cue-ball to a spot far distant from the ball on (the ball your opponent must play at), generally the other end of the table. This is known as a 'safety shot'.

Suppose several reds are left, and there is no scoring stroke discernible. Here it is policy to direct the cue-ball to part of the table remote from the reds. The mere fact that it is now far away from the ball on handicaps your opponent. This type of stroke is a constant feature of the game.

After the shot shown in the diagram, the opponent must strike the cue-ball when it is close up against the cushion, which makes accurate cueing and direction difficult. In this position his only course is to execute a safety shot himself; but none of the reds is now easy to contact, and he will probably come to grief over the stroke, leaving his ball among the reds. It will also probably be in a favourable position for his opponent to pot several balls. This 'return to baulk' stroke is productive of many a good opening, and is especially favoured in the early stages of the game when the table is crowded. In this case, with no reds favourably placed for potting, the player chose instead to execute the 'return to baulk' or 'bottom cushion' stroke.

The 'shot to nothing'

In the early and middle stages of the game, a player can gain an important advantage with the so-called 'shot to nothing'. If he succeeds in potting a red while executing the return to baulk, he is then on a colour, and can take the chance to snooker his opponent behind a colour lying in the baulk area. He can achieve this by creeping slowly up to the colour, though he must hit it or the stroke is a miss and forfeits points. The diagrams on page 30 show an example of this stroke.

In the first stroke, the shot to nothing, the player pots red and returns to the baulk area. In the second, where an attempt to pot yellow from such a distance might be risky, he prefers to snooker behind green. The advantage follows from the previous stroke, in which the red was potted.

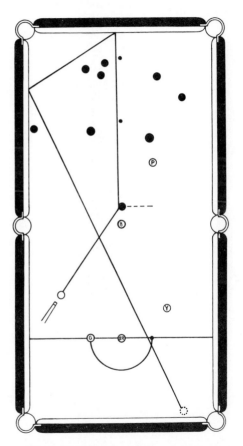

Safety shot

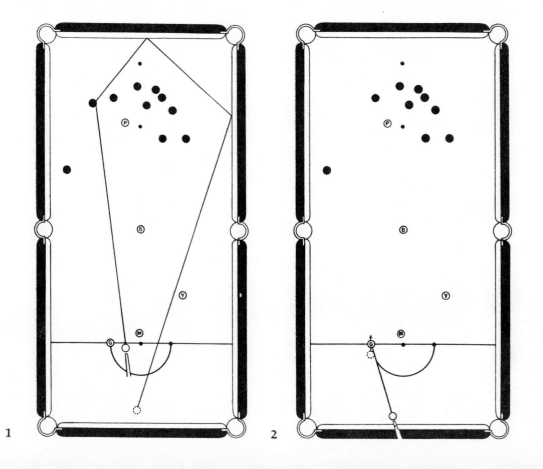

The 'shot to nothing'   1   2

Nominating a ball

A player nominates a ball by indicating he is on it – in other words, that he intends to hit it. Normally he need only nominate when some doubt exists. For instance, if he has potted a red and then aims in the direction of two colours very close to one another, the referee cannot tell which of them he intends to hit unless he nominates one.

If a player is snookered after a foul, he is on any ball he cares to nominate. If he is on a red but is unable to hit it directly on both sides, he may nominate a colour as a red. This is generally referred to as a 'free ball'. The player must hit the nominated ball or it is a foul. The nominated, or 'free', ball acquires the value of the ball on. For instance, a player who nominates black for a red scores only one point if he pots the black. In the same way, after the reds are disposed of, the player may nominate any other colour when he is snookered by a foul. If the 'free' ball is potted, it must be re-spotted in any case. If the player uses the 'free' or nominated ball to snooker, he commits a foul, except when only pink and black are left on the table.

If the player pots the nominated ball he scores the value of the ball on, as stated. If he fails to pot the nominated ball, but pots the ball on, he scores its value: for instance, nominating green as red, the player fails to pot green but pots red. He scores one point and continues his break. If he pots both he scores only the value of the ball on, and continues. In this situation only the nominated ball must be re-spotted. Whatever happens the player must first *hit* the nominated ball.

Cue-ball touching

If the cue-ball is touching a ball that is not on, the player must play away from it without moving it.

If the cue-ball is touching a ball that *is* on, the player must also play away from it without moving it, but he need not hit another ball.

Common phrases

A 'black ball game'. A game in which the scores are close enough for the value of the black ball (seven) to decide the game. If the difference is six or less, the first score or forfeit ends the game. If the difference is seven, and the scores then become equal, the black is spotted and the players draw lots for the choice of playing from hand.

'Wanting a snooker'. This means a player cannot win except by making his opponent forfeit points. For example, suppose A leads B by 50 to 30 points, and only blue, pink and black remain (18 points). If B pots all three balls his score will be 48, so he will still lose. However, if he can lay a snooker and cause his opponent to miss, go in-off etc, he will have the benefit of the points forfeited by his opponent. For instance, if he achieves a snooker on the blue – the next ball on in the prescribed sequence of colours – and if his opponent fails to hit it, he will be awarded five points.

With the remaining three balls (18 points plus 5) he will be able to win 53–50; provided, of course, that A does not score again. In this situation he therefore 'wants one snooker'.

'*Taking the colours*'. When all the reds have been potted only the colours remain. To 'take the colours' means to pot them in one break in the correct sequence from yellow to black.

'*Set*' or '*plant*'. These two terms have become practically synonymous. Generally speaking they apply to a position in which two reds are touching one another. In such a position one of the balls can be potted by contacting, in the one case, the ball nearer the pocket, or, in the other, the further one. In the first instance a squeeze between the cue-ball and the second object-ball achieves the pot; in the other, correct contact on the ball further from the pocket gives the necessary direction to the one nearer the pocket.

Fouls exclusive to snooker
(For fouls common to both snooker and billiards, see p.34.)

A player must not:

(a) Direct the cue-ball into a pocket ('go in-off') whether it strikes another ball, or balls, or not.

(b) Pot a ball out of the correct order (i.e. pot one that is not on): for instance, by potting one red, then another red, instead of a colour.

(c) Fail to hit the ball he has nominated after a foul by his opponent.

(d) Move a ball which is touching the cue-ball, instead of playing away from it without moving it.

(e) Strike two balls simultaneously unless both are red balls, or one is the ball nominated and the other is the ball on.

(f) Snooker with the ball nominated after a foul, unless only pink and black remain on the table.

(g) Commit a foul after potting a red before nominating or attempting to play a colour. The penalty is seven points.

After a foul stroke by his opponent, a player may play from the position left or ask his opponent to play the next stroke. If he fouls again, he can again be asked to play the next stroke.

Penalties
The penalties for the various fouls are given in the official Rule Book, but as a general principle the penalties for most fouls are calculated according to the values of the balls involved in the foul, and the player forfeits the value of the highest. As the minimum penalty is four points, it follows that the forfeit value of the red, yellow and green balls will be four in each case, not one, two and three respectively. There is also a rule stating that the first impact governs all strokes, but this does not always apply if two fouls are involved in the stroke.

Here are some examples:

(a) A player on red strikes black. Seven points forfeit (or, as it is commonly known, 'seven away').

(b) A player on black strikes red. Seven points forfeit. Both here and in (a) above the black value, seven, is the higher and therefore determines the forfeit.

(c) A player on red misses red and strikes blue. Five away. (The blue value, five, is higher than the red forfeit value, four.)

(d) Player on blue misses it and strikes the green. The cue-ball, still moving, contacts pink, which enters a pocket, and the player then fouls black with his cue. In this case the forfeit is seven.

(e) Player pots yellow, and then fouls pink with his cue after the cue-ball has stopped. The penalty is six points, and the yellow is re-spotted.

(f) The player snookers with the nominated ball (free ball). The penalty is the value of the ball on. So if the player chooses black as his nominated ball after a foul, when the green is on, and then snookers with the black, his penalty is only four points.

(g) Black is the ball on, but after the player has hit it, it cannons onto the blue and pots it. The penalty is seven points, the highest value involved.

(h) Player is on red, and hits it, but his cue-ball goes on to strike black and then goes 'in-off' (into a pocket). Penalty is four points: first impact (which governs all strokes) was on the red, for which the penalty is the minimum, four.

(i) Player on a red is snookered after a foul. He nominates black, fails to hit it and strikes a red, also potting black. Penalty is four points because black, the nominated ball, acquired the value of the red for which it was nominated, and therefore also acquires its penalty value.

Fouls common to both billiards and snooker

A player must not:
(a) Push the cue-ball with the cue, instead of striking it.
(b) Force a ball (or balls) off the table.
(c) Play a stroke with *both* feet off the floor.
(d) Play a stroke before the balls have come to rest.
(e) Touch the ball other than with the cue-tip (for instance with his hand, or his clothes).
(f) Touch the ball with the cue-tip before he has delivered his stroke.
(g) Use the 'jump shot', by which the cue-ball is made to leap over another ball by hitting it very low down.
(h) Use a dead ball to test whether a ball will pass another, or go on a spot, or for any other purpose.

Variants

Volunteer Snooker
Volunteer is a variation of the normal snooker game; it is easy to play and appeals to those who have no wish to master the real game.

The balls are set out exactly as in snooker. The difference lies in the way the balls are potted. In snooker the player's task is to pot a red and then a colour until all the reds are potted, when he must pot the colours in rotation. In Volunteer Snooker, after potting a red and then a colour, the player may take another colour out of its proper order. This colour must be named, and is then said to have been 'volunteered' by the player. Suppose, for example, you have potted a red and the pink. You may now declare, or volunteer, any other colour you wish by naming it. This ball, of course, will be the easiest one to pot after the pink. If you fail to pot your volunteered ball you forfeit its value (seven if black, six if pink, five if blue, and so on) to your opponent. Naturally, this risk gives the game an extra element of expectancy. However, if you pot the volunteered ball three times in succession in the same turn, it remains off the table until the next stroke. For this next stroke a red or any colour may be chosen, and it is 'free': there is no penalty if you fail to pot it.

You may not volunteer a ball until you have lawfully potted a red in each visit or turn at the table. If a player who lawfully pockets the last red ball pockets any pool ball by his next stroke, the pool ball is re-spotted. A red ball is always free; you may always play on it. If the reds are all off the table, then the next ball to be played is the ball which is on.

Reckless play can be expensive, and it is obviously unwise to volunteer a ball that is difficult to pot. It is better to take the easier chances. As in snooker, the player must have the ability to pot with confidence.

Apart from the volunteering element, the game is subject to the same rules as snooker, and the player must know the rules of both games to play properly.

The rules of Volunteer Snooker are included with those of Billiards and Snooker in the official handbook and rules published by the Billiards and Snooker Control Council. These are worth buying.

Russian Pool

This game is also known as Indian Pool, Toad-in-the-Hole or Slosh, and is another of the many additional games that add to the enjoyment of the billiard table. It is a combination of billiards and snooker, and its 'free-scoring' possibilities make it a pleasant diversion, especially for players who are not very skilled at either billiards or snooker.

Five balls are used in the game: white (the cue-ball), yellow, green, blue and black. Black goes on the billiard spot (where the red is placed at the beginning of billiards), blue on the centre spot, green on the left-hand and yellow on the right-hand corner of the 'D'. The ball values are as follows: black, when potted or the object of a losing hazard, nine points; blue, seven; green, five; yellow, three. The scoring of the game is by winning or losing hazards (pots or in-offs), scoring as explained, and also by cannons (which score two points). Consecutive direct cannons on the same two balls are limited to twenty-five; after this the player must make a hazard or a direct cannon, that is, one from ball to ball. He may also continue his break after twenty-five cannons if he makes a direct cannon in conjunction with a hazard, or a cannon in which at least one of the balls is different from those of the twenty-five cannons referred to. With the high ball values for hazards, scoring can be quite high compared with billiards or snooker. For example, by cannoning from black to blue, combined with pocketing black in the top pocket and blue in the centre pocket, you can score eighteen points in one stroke. However, you may not pot the balls into *any* pocket. Black may be potted only into the two top pockets, blue only in the two centre pockets, and green and yellow only into the two bottom pockets. This rule also applies to losing hazards (in-offs). Not more than three consecutive winning hazards of the same ball off the same spot may be made without conjunction of another score. The game is started with the black ball being struck by direct contact.

The cannon is a valuable stroke for scoring, even though its value is only two points. Many opportunities for cannon sequences recur, and skill at cannon play is a valuable asset in the game. A good scoring sequence can be created by manoeuvring the balls in a cannon sequence towards a pocket that permits a losing or winning hazard. The game gives scope for positional play; it is useful to concentrate on controlling your first ball when you are making a cannon, and the possibility of manoeuvring from cannons to hazards is fascinating. But if the scores are high, so are the penalties, and clearly there is little point in achieving high scores at the cost of high penalties from mistakes.

Russian Pool is sometimes played with an extra ball, pink, which is spotted on the pyramid spot and is known as the 'rover'. With pink, winning or losing hazards may be made in any pocket and score six points. It may also, of course, be used for cannon play (two points). The aim of the game, as with billiards and snooker, is to score more points up to a mutually agreed figure.

Golf

Golf is often played by two, three or four players. The six colours together with one red ball and the white are used in pairs: black and pink, blue and brown, green and yellow, and red and white. In each case the first-named ball of the pair is used as the cue-ball.

The players draw for the pairs they will use. The player who draws the red and white is first to strike, followed by green, blue and black. The object-ball is placed on the centre spot and the striker plays from hand. The aim is to pot the object-ball into every pocket, starting with the top left-hand pocket and proceeding clockwise round the table to finish with the left centre. After the object-ball has been potted it is replaced on the centre spot, and the cue-ball is played from wherever it has come to rest while the player continues his turn.

To miss, go in-off or pot a ball out of sequence is a foul stroke, and the player forfeits one pocket, or 'hole'. After a foul stroke the two balls are removed from the table till the player's next turn. Any balls other than the cue or object ball that are disturbed during a foul stroke are replaced in their original position.

As you can see, accurate control of the cue-ball is essential to pot the object-ball into the correct pocket. Accurate control of both balls is needed to snooker one of the opponents or deny him access to his pocket.

Printed by Swannack, Brown & Co., Ltd., Hull, England